The Power Of Instagram Marketing

- *for Local Businesses*

25 Things You Should Know

By Varinder Grewal

Table of Contents

About the Author

Varinder Grewal has been working with local businesses as well as national and international businesses since 2006. His company provides consultancy, marketing technology & marketing strategy.

The internet has allowed the small business owner and new start ups to punch above their weight and with the right strategy, techniques and sometimes technology, there is no excuse not to take on any competitor regardless of their size! But with the fast moving internet, you have to be on the ball all of the time, only then will you be in a category of one and not have to compete in the "bargain basement".

Read the book, take action and watch your business explode with Instagram! And when you're ready to take it up a notch, contact Varinder at:

vinny@socialmediaactive.com

Is Instagram free to use for businesses?

It's the first question business owners ask when they're considering any new type of marketing. Or, well, when buying anything for their business. The good news here is that Instagram is 100% free for individuals and businesses to use. And, if you're thinking that they let you sign up for free to later hit you with all kinds of added expenses, think again. All of Instagram's features are free for businesses to use, too!

Why should I use Instagram for my business?

Even after finding out it's free to use, many business owners still look for reasons *not* to use something. After all, who needs one more project added to their to-do list? But there are several reasons why business owners should stop with this kind of reasoning and really take a look at all the benefits Instagram offers to business owners.

Consider first that Instagram has over 700 million users all around the world. So any business can use Instagram to build an audience and convert them into paying customers. This jaw-dropping number proves that when businesses are looking for their next 100 customers, there's a pretty good chance that they can find them on the third-largest social network platform that's available worldwide.

Another astounding fact is that over 50 percent of all brands are currently using Instagram to promote their business. This means that even if your business isn't currently on Instagram, there's a very good chance that your competitors are. And you have no way of beating them on this point if your business isn't on Instagram. Even if your competitors are not on Instagram, there's a very good chance that they soon will be. And by signing up today and taking part in it, you can beat them to the punch.

But, maybe you are on Instagram – as a social network, not as a marketing platform for your business. When that's the case, you need to consider that engagement with brands on Instagram is 10 times higher than Facebook, 54 times higher than Pinterest, and 84 times higher than Twitter.

Engagement should always be a business owner's first priority when it comes to any social media. It's the amount of likes, comments, and followers your profile receives. In short, it's how interested your customers and potential customers are. And when you know that Instagram is the opportunity for so much more engagement than what you're currently getting on other social media platforms, don't be surprised if in the future you consider abandoning those other social networks in favor of Instagram.

So why should your business be on Instagram? Because Instagram marketing is clearly the way forward.

Should I use Instagram for business when I'm in a serious industry?

So maybe you're a doctor, or a banker, or a lawyer, or a real estate agent. And you've heard all kinds of stories about how Instagram is used by millennials and other young people to take snapshots of their food and post selfies. Does your business really have a place within it?

In short: YES! Many marketers think that social media and in particular, Instagram, is only created for industries that target young people, but this is simply not true. The first reason is that, even if you're only attracting those young people, they still use those industries that are considered to be more serious. They still need to use a bank, they still need to visit doctors, and they're still buying homes and properties.

Secondly, while it's true that Instagram has become to be known as 'the social media platform of millennials,' they are not in fact, the only ones using it. Women over the age of 35 make up a huge demographic of Instagram and others are using it, too.

The secret is not *which* social media platform you use, but *how* you use it. And being one of the largest and fastest-growing social media platforms in the world, there's no reason any business owner should consider not marketing on Instagram.

Do I need to have a Facebook account *and* an Instagram account to run ads on Instagram?

As a business owner, you may find that social media is getting too 'busy' for you. There are simply too many and keeping up with all of them can become a full-time job that keeps you from the very business you're trying to promote with them. For this reason, many business owners try to limit the amount of platforms they're on. Facebook, a social media platform that is often thought of as a place for people to post what they had for lunch or what they're doing this afternoon, may be one of those that you're considering leaving. But, you shouldn't.

In 2012, Facebook purchased Instagram for a whopping $1 billion; $300 million in cash and the rest in Facebook stock. And ever since then, Facebook and Instagram have been very closely intertwined.

Currently, it seems as though any business owner that wants to run Instagram ads must not only have a Facebook account but also a Facebook Page for their business. Business owners can however, run Facebook ads without having an Instagram account, but there are some downsides to this.

The first is that you won't be able to reply to any comments on your Instagram ads, which could potentially lose you customers as they'll simply think you don't care enough to answer. Your ads will also appear under your Facebook Page's name and while this may not be a completely bad thing, Instagram users won't be able to click on it, which could lose you customers and traffic.

How can I create a great Instagram profile?

The most valuable part of any social media account is the profile. It tells other Instagram users exactly what the business is, the services and products that you offer, and where you're located. There are three aspects to any Instagram profile: username, website, and bio. Each of these has to be filled out properly in order to ensure that the profile as a whole isn't just interesting, but that it also conveys to users what the business does and how it helps customers.

A username on Instagram is also the name the account, similar to handles on Twitter. It's also what follows the '@' symbol that customers will use to search for a specific company, or to tag them within the app. Generally speaking, when businesses are setting up their profile, they'll want to use their business name or the handle that they use on other social media networks.

Adding a website URL to a profile is of huge importance in Instagram. Because Instagram does not allow links in posts and comments, this is really the only place where business owners can direct users and potential customers to their website to learn more. And really, is there any type of marketing that you would consider *not* adding your website URL to?

Writing the bio is where most business owners tend to get tripped up when creating an Instagram profile, but it's the most important part. This is where you state what the purpose of your company is, show the voice your brand uses, and establishes credibility. This is where business owners can create custom hashtags for their business and let users know what they'll be sharing on Instagram. It's also a good idea to keep creativity in mind when creating this bio, as it will stand out among the crowd and make users more interested in learning more about your company.

And while you want to let users know as much as possible about your business, it's important to keep this bio to four lines or less. This will allow them to see it without scrolling, and it will also allow them to see the full images that you post – also while scrolling.

What is the best time of day to post?

When considering when to post, it's important to remember two things. The first is that Instagram users have to use a phone in order to access the app. It is after all, an app and not a website. For this reason, there is a smaller chance that they'll be browsing it at work, like they may with Facebook and Twitter. Instead, they'll most likely pull out their phone and look at Instagram during their downtime.

For this reason, multiple studies show that the best time to post to Instagram in order to be seen by the most viewers is from 5:00 p.m. to 6:00 p.m. on weekdays, and during the weekends. There is also evidence to show that posting late at night is also very effective, as this is a time when people are still on their downtime, but there are also not a lot of other users posting.

But there is one more thing to remember, and that's the fact that not every strategy will work for every business. For this reason, it's important to test, test, and test again at different times of the day and on different days of the week. See what gets the most likes when, what engages users the most, and when posting seems to be most effective. This is really the only way to know when it's best for *your* business to post.

How do Instagram hashtags work?

Hashtags are becoming a huge part of social networking. They began on Twitter and are now starting to reach out to all of them. Hashtags are a word or phrase preceded by the pound symbol. So the hashtag for the word 'hashtag' would be '#hashtag.'

Hashtags are useful for a number of different purposes. First, they allow users who don't even follow someone to still see their posts and pictures. So, if a real estate agent in New York wanted to attract more Instagram users they may post a picture of one of the properties they have for sale. And in the caption for that picture they may include a hashtag with it such as #housesforsaleNYC or #NYCrealty so people can find it, no matter who they follow on Instagram.

But hashtags can be useful for more than just Instagram searches, and that's when businesses take advantage of making branded hashtags. These are hashtags that may not be popular or common, but are relevant to a specific marketing campaign the business is running. So that real estate agency may ask followers to post pictures of their own home, whether it's for sale or not, using the hashtag #thisismyhome or #homeoftheweek. This can increase engagement and help the business get more followers, as well as more customers.

How many hashtags should I use?

Once you understand just how useful, and how plentiful, hashtags can be, it can be tempting to include as many hashtags as you can possibly think of. While Instagram does place a limit of 30 hashtags on any individual post, there's a good reason businesses should stick with the general rule of thumb which is 5 hashtags.

When a post has too many hashtags following it, so much gets lost. The idea behind the caption gets lost, and the overall effect of the image gets lost too. Too many hashtags simply makes your post look bad. And while it can open the door to new opportunities, as more people will be able to find your post through Instagram search, it's going to give your existing followers a bad experience; and that could actually lose you followers.

Of course, once in a while you can use more than five hashtags. But try not to make it a habit.

Can I create photos on my computer?

So you understand that Instagram is an app that you can download to your phone. And you may understand that you'll have to use that phone in order to write and publish your posts. And you undoubtedly know that you also have a camera on your phone that will help you take the pictures that will be uploaded to your profile. But does this mean that's the only way to create photos for Instagram? What if you have a great photo editor on your laptop that you love using and want to use that to upload photos?

You can, no matter what type of phone you're using to post to Instagram. Android users can simply plug their phone into their computer and upload the picture from their computer to their phone. And Apple users can simply connect to iCloud through their computer, upload the photo, and then use their phone to access it.

While the photo does need to be on a smartphone before it can be uploaded to Instagram, there's no reason why that picture must always start on the phone before being edited or uploaded to the social media platform.

How can I get more Instagram followers?

Everyone wants followers on social media; that's the whole point of it. And businesses especially want more followers because without them, they're talking to nobody and not gaining any more exposure or possible customers. So the big question is: how can you get them?

Start by following other people and commenting on their posts. But, instead of just doing this blindly as so many do on their personal accounts, look for accounts that have the same interests as you and that have the type of followers you want. Also try to be the last comment made, as anyone else who sees the post will also see your comment; and you'll open yourself up to a whole new world of opportunities than you would by allowing your comment to get lost in the mix.

In order for this to work however, you need to be genuine with your comments and make sure that they are interesting, useful, and perhaps even show off some of your personality.

Another very effective way to gain more followers is to share engaging videos. Video can be a great way for businesses to build trust with their followers and reach new audiences. In addition to that, people like videos more than they like still photos because they find them more interesting and more fun to watch. This will increase the amount users engage with your videos in the way of liking them and commenting on them. And, with Instagram giving a higher priority to posts that have higher engagement rates, it also means that more people will see your video, which in turn will get you more followers.

Running a contest is also a great way to get more followers and promote your business at the same time. There are a number of ways to run contests on Instagram, including partnering up with another business or Instagram influencer to do it. Give away rewards to users that follow both businesses as part of the contest and also tag their friends in the comments. They'll have to follow you in order to get in on the fun, and you'll automatically increase the number of followers you have.

Can I buy followers on Instagram?

There are a lot of businesses out there that make a lot of money by offering to sell followers to businesses that are willing to buy them. In fact, for as little as $7 you could immediately have up to 500 Instagram followers. And while this is very tempting to many businesses that want to quickly increase the number of followers they have, it's a practice that shouldn't be used.

The first reason for this is that the followers you get will have nothing to do with you; and they won't care about you. People follow businesses on Instagram because they have an interest in your business. They're likely to ask questions about upcoming promotions, become involved in contests, and like images that you share of your business. Followers that are purchased won't do any of this because they're simply a number. And in most cases, they are either dud accounts created by those who sold them, or their robots that don't engage at all with other user accounts.

Another good reason not to buy followers is because your engagement rate will drop. Instagram will notice this and will no longer make your posts a priority, meaning fewer people will see them – even if they follow you. When you have a lot of followers but you keep posting and there's very little engagement on those posts, Instagram will think there's nothing of value in your posts to other users. And they will lower the ranking of those posts so they won't show up in the feed of other users.

Lastly, purchasing followers has a serious downside should genuine users ever find out about it. They'll take this to mean that your profile can't get users on its own simply by posting engaging content that's interesting to users.

Customers love transparency these days and there's nothing less transparent than trying to promote yourself as having a lot of followers when you don't. These fake profiles are very easy to find just by taking a good look at their bio and once your genuine followers find out you've purchased followers, you're going to have a lot fewer followers in general.

Who should I follow on Instagram?

It's true that following others is a great way to get more followers for your business. But who you follow is important, so make sure you're not just clicking through Instagram following any user you happen to come across.

First and foremost, start following people by following only those people that interest you. After all, this is your Instagram account and you're going to be the one scrolling through images to interact with so make sure those images are going to be things that actually interest you. Start by searching not just for your family and friends but also brands, celebrities, photographers, artists, and even cute animals and look at the content they're sharing. If it interests you, follow them.

Next, start looking for companies and brands within your industry that seem to know everything about using Instagram. Watch what they do, how they engage, what works, and what doesn't. There's a lot to be learned by doing this and once you start following them, you'll always be able to see what they do well.

After following the big players and those who interest you, you'll probably wonder whether or not you should follow your customers. And the answer is: sometimes. You should absolutely follow customers that are dedicated and are always raving about you and your company. By engaging with their posts you'll show that you care about them too, and that will go a long way in promoting your business. But be careful about how many customers you follow. If a customer doesn't post things that are highly relevant to your business or doesn't interest you, and they also don't engage a lot with your account, it's okay not to follow them.

If your business has any partners or associates, you should absolutely follow them on Instagram. It will show that you support them, and it will also give you a chance to see what they're doing.

While it's important to know who to follow, it's just as important to know who not to follow. And while it can seem nice to follow everyone who follows you, it's a practice that shouldn't be done. It will come across as inauthentic and can actually allow spam accounts into your Instagram feed, which can really throw your profile for a loop. Before following anyone, verify their Instagram account by making sure they have a complete bio, actual videos or photos, and real engagement and conversations. Their Instagram account should also be more than a few weeks old, which you can check by seeing how many posts they have and how far back they go.

And while it's okay to follow someone, it's just as okay to unfollow them later on. Maybe they start creating content that just doesn't resonate with you, or maybe they eventually unfollow you and there's just no advantage to you following them anymore. Whatever you do, never follow anyone just to get a follow back and then unfollow them. That is considered to be bad Instagram form, and the followers who are still watching you will likely notice.

Why are people unfollowing me?

One thing that will never change about Instagram is the fact that followers have very unpredictable behavior. You may see a surge in followers one day only to find that number seriously depleted the next day. In many cases, there's nothing you can do about this. But if you find that your number of followers is steadily decreasing and you're not getting a lot of new followers, there could be a couple of reasons for it.

Inconsistent posting is one reason why people will unfollow you. This doesn't mean you have to post every day, but if you've consistently posted great content every week and then stop posting for three or four weeks, people might think that you're gone for good and stop following you. However, if you're posting too often and always posting a bunch of pictures at once, you'll clog up people's feeds and that could be seen as annoying. Instead, spread your posts out for maximum impact and engagement.

You may also lose followers if you're not engaging with your followers at all. People like to follow others on Instagram but what they like even more is when it's a reciprocal relationship. They don't want to be the ones commenting and liking your posts all the time; they want you to like and comment their posts too.

While giveaways can be good, don't be surprised if you suddenly lose a number of followers right after they've ended. Many people will start following a company just to take part in their giveaways or contests and then unfollow them when that time is over. This doesn't mean you shouldn't run contests and giveaways; it just means losing followers is a by-product of doing it.

Lastly, if you have a lot of spam bots following you, you may suddenly see that your number of followers goes down one day. This is because Instagram regularly tries to get rid of spam accounts and fake profiles. If this happens occasionally but not that often, it's nothing to worry about and isn't a sign you've done anything wrong on Instagram. But if it happens too often, it may be a sign of something more.

Why has Instagram suddenly blocked me from following other people?

It happens. You're on Instagram, happily clicking all those 'Follow' buttons under user accounts, and all of a sudden you can't do it anymore. You're not aware of any follower limits Instagram has placed on accounts, and you don't think you've done anything wrong. And you haven't.

But, there is a chance that you've followed too many people for that hour. In order to stop spammers and Instagram bots, Instagram only allows users to follow people and send follow requests to 200 users per hour. This is a lot and if you run into this problem, there's a chance you're following too many people to begin with, since you will after all, have to keep track of those people you follow in your feed.

If it happens, and you think you still can keep up with all those people, just wait an hour or so. You'll be able to follow people again after that time.

Should I have a personal or business account?

Facebook is fairly easy. You have a personal profile and a Page, of which you are the admin. And Twitter's not that much more complicated; just use a handle that clearly identifies your business and voila! It's a business account. But Instagram is a little bit different. You have the choice of running a personal account or business account; and both are free, so that's not going to help you come to a decision. So how do you decide? It all comes down to what you want to do with your Instagram account, and how simple you want to keep things.

If you want to really know everything there is about your posts including reach, profile views, mentions and more, you'll need to choose a business account. Instagram Insights provide just that – valuable insights that will let you see not only the engagement on your post but also things about the demographics of people that liked them; their gender, location, age, and the time and days that they're most active on Instagram. That can be invaluable to a business.

And if you want to be able to promote posts, particularly those ones telling users about a promotion or new product, you'll need a business account on Instagram to do it. While this is something that in the past had to be done through Facebook, Instagram has made it easier for businesses to do right within the app; and it's a real timesaver.

Perhaps the biggest bonus that comes from having a business account on Instagram though, is the fact that it's so much easier for people to contact you. With a button right on your profile they'll never have to go searching for it again. And that's a great thing, because most won't.

However, if you're already on Instagram using a personal account and you've built a nice little following, engaging with other's posts and having them engage with yours, you may fear that switching to a business account will seem less personal and inauthentic. The fear is real here, and it can happen. If you think that it could happen to you, stick with the personal account.

On Instagram, it also used to be that posts got shown in chronological order. No one post was given a preference over another. But Instagram is a business too, and with its new algorithm, some smaller businesses are finding that not as many people see their posts and pictures anymore. This is because with so many big businesses and corporations using Instagram business accounts, and paying big bucks in advertising, Instagram gives them preference, pushing the posts of the smaller guys to the bottom of the pile. If you want to switch to a business profile but think this may hurt you, try switching just for a little while and see if your posts get more attention and engagement. If not, just switch back to your personal account.

How can I make the most out of Instagram for my business?

This question comes when using any kind of social media platform and Instagram is no different. And truthfully, there are a lot of ways it can be done. Use hashtags, especially popular ones like #ThrowbackThursday, run a contest, and share behind-the-scenes photos of your company (people love those!) But really, it comes down to two things.

The first is to post consistently. This doesn't mean posting five times a day, or even posting every day. But whenever you choose to post, make sure that it's a regular thing. Don't post every day for a month and then suddenly not post for two months. People will become disinterested and will stop following you.

Secondly, if you're using image or video to show your product, don't just show the product itself. Instead, show people using the product so that people can imagine how it would work for them and how it could make their life so much easier.

How do I know if I have high engagement rates?

So three people have liked that photo you posted at lunchtime and it's not even the end of the day. That must mean you have a high engagement rate, right? But does it? You don't know what's happening on other people's profiles and pictures so how can you be sure? Luckily, the people of Track Maven studies Fortune 500 companies, those with some of the highest engagement rates, and came up with a simple equation to figure out your engagement rate. All you have to do is multiply the number of followers you have by 0.037.

This means that if you have 1,000 followers, you should aim for 37 likes and comments on any one post. If you have 500 followers, the aim should be for 19 likes and comments; and if you have 5,000 followers, posts should have about 185 likes and comments. While this is by no means an exact science, it will let you know whether or not your engagement rate is even close to the big players and may tell you to analyze your posts if there's very little engagement to see where you're going wrong.

Why should I use Instagram ads?

You may think that simply being very smart about posting is enough to get you more customers and open the door to new opportunities. And you're probably not entirely wrong. But if you want to boost those efforts, and see even more profit for it, Instagram ads are a great way to do it.

Instagram is pretty new to the ad game, have run them only since 2015. But in the two years since that's happened, Instagram ads have driven more than one billion user actions. And as of last year, there were 500,000 advertisers on Instagram. That statistic alone is enough to make any business want to advertise on Instagram. After all, if you're not it's likely your competition is, giving them the edge.

But it's not just businesses that are on Instagram, customers are too! As one of the fastest growing social media platforms, Instagram is truly where the people are; and isn't that something you're looking for in any marketing campaign? So you can advertise to the masses?

Those users have the intent to buy. Instagram performed their own study that showed 60 percent of users say they learn about new products and services through Instagram. And of those, 75 percent say they take action such as visiting the business' website, searching, or telling a friend about the Instagram post. And these are all great reasons to use Instagram ads!

Perhaps the reason Instagram's study saw so many people taking action is because Instagram ads are so highly targeted. They use Facebook's advertising system, which is known for being highly targeted and honing in on user's location, age, interests, behaviors, and more.

So the big reason why you should use Instagram ads for your business? Simply put, it gets results.

Are Instagram ads more effective for some businesses than they are for others?

Here you probably expect the answer to be, "No! Any business should advertise on Instagram!" But while any business *can* advertise on the social media platform, it doesn't necessarily mean that all businesses should. But, certainly most businesses should.

First, determine who you're trying to target. Contrary to popular belief, the largest demographic that uses Instagram are those between 18 and 34 years old (26%) while millennials follow behind them (23%). And in the U.S. 38% of females are more likely to use Instagram than males at 26%.

And your industry matters, too. The most popular industries across Instagram are fashion and beauty, food, TV and films, hobbies, and music. If you're in one of these industries, you need to be on Instagram. If you're not, ask yourself if you can create visual content that blends into your users' feed; and if you can create visual storytelling with your posts. If you can, you need to start using Instagram ads today.

If not, try testing the waters on Instagram before spending any money on ads. If you get high engagement rates on your posts, go ahead and start spending some of your advertising budget on Instagram. You might just be surprised at the results you see.

What are the different types of ads on Instagram?

One of the best things about Instagram ads is that there are so many different ways to do it with so many different types of ads. So, let's take a quick look at each.

Single image ads are the most common type of ad on both Instagram and Facebook. This ad includes only an image, ad copy, and a call to action button.

Carousel ads on the other hand, allow you to include up to ten images or videos in a single ad. Users just flip through to see them by swiping right or left and they're a great way to tell a story within an ad.

Slideshow ads are very similar to carousel ads in that they can include up to ten images or videos. The difference with slideshow ads is that they can also include music with them.

Video ads are great at grabbing a user's attention as they scroll through their feed. They're a fun way to share a promotion, tell a story, or show how a product works.

Lead ads are just that – ads that are great at collecting leads; but it doesn't take them off Instagram to do it. With these ads, the user is just taken to a new page that includes a lead form asking for their contact details. These are a great way for businesses to build up their contact lists and, as the name implies, get more leads!

Instagram Stories can be used as an ad, either with just an image or with a video. These will appear in user's Stories feeds and can be a fun and engaging way to get your ad in front of people. With the video option, businesses are given 15 seconds for their ad space.

Are there any guidelines for Instagram ads?

Sometimes just knowing the specs can help you determine what kind of ad you want to run. After all, if you're excited about running a video ad you're not going to choose the single image format. Below are the specs for each ad type, to help you make the choice of which one will work best for you.

Single image ad

Caption: up to 125 characters
Media type: image
Recommended image size: 1080 x 1080 pixels or 1200 x 628 pixels (the typical Facebook ad image size)
Image format: .jpg or .png
Max. file siize: 30 MB

Carousel ads

Caption: up to 125 characters
Media type: image or video
Recommended image/video resolution: min. 600 x 600 pixels, max. 1080 x 1080 pixels
Image format: .jpg or .png
Minimum number of cards: 2
Maximum number of cards: 10
Image ratio: 1:1
Video aspect ratio: 1:1
Minimum video length: 3 seconds
Maximum video length: 60 seconds
Video thumbnail image ratio: Should match the aspect ratio of your video. If not, thumbnail auto resize is available.

Slideshow ads

Caption: up to 125 characters
Media type: images + soundtrack
Image duration: up to 50sec per image
Image size: min. 600 x 600 pixels, max. 1080 x 1080 pixels. If you use images of different sizes, your slideshow will be cropped to be square.
Music file format: WAV, MP3, M4A, FLAC and OGG. You must have all legal rights necessary to use the song!

Video ads

Caption: up to 125 characters
Media type: video
Recommended video resolution: 600 x 600 pixels (square) or 600 x 315 pixels (landscape)
Aspect Ratio: 1:1 (square) or 1.9:1 (landscape)
Minimum resolution: 600 x 600 pixels
Maximum resolution: 1080 x 1080 pixels
Minimum length: 3 seconds
Maximum length: 60 seconds
Maximum size: 4GB
Frame rate: 30fps max
File type: .mp4 container
Video: H.264 video compression, high profile preferred, square pixels, fixed frame rate, progressive scan
Audio: Stereo AAC audio compression, 128kbps + preferred

Lead ads

Caption: up to 125 characters
Media type: image
Recommended ad image size: 1080 x 1080 pixels or 1200 x 628 pixels (the typical Facebook ad image size)
Image format: .jpg or .png

Max. file size: 30 MB
Other requirements: Privacy policy

Stories image ads

Caption: not currently available. Any text must be part of
the image file
Format: Full screen vertical ad (9:16)
Recommended Resolution: 1080 x 1920
Minimum Resolution: 600 x 1067
File types: .jpg or .png
Max. image size: 30MB
Photo content: visible for 5 seconds

Stories video ads

Caption: not currently available. Any text must be part of
the image file
Format: Full screen vertical ad (9:16)
Recommended Resolution: 1080 x 1920
Minimum Resolution: 600 x 1067
File types: mp4 or .mov
Max. video size: 4GB
Max. video lengtht: 15 seconds
Recommended Video Codecs: h.264, VP8
Recommended Audio Codecs: AAC, Vorbis

What are the benefits of running a contest on Instagram?

There are a lot of businesses that don't like to give stuff away, but running a contest on Instagram is a great way to promote your business and get it more exposure. And you don't have to give away thousands of dollars' worth in prizes in order to do it.

Running an Instagram contest is a fun and easy way to get more followers while promoting your business and interacting with your followers. They'll win cool stuff, some of which may even have your logo on it so they'll think of you in the future when they need your product or service, and you'll get the word out about your business to even more people.

And the prize doesn't even have to be something that you're currently selling, but something you create just for the contest. If you're a real estate agent for instance, you can create a report about how to negotiate an offer to purchase; or what home inspections are and why they're so important. People love free stuff and while the prize you give away has to have some value, it doesn't mean you have to clear your stock shelves just to run an Instagram contest.

What type of contest should I run?

Maybe you have no idea what kind of contest can be run on Instagram. Or maybe you know that there are so many different types of contests, you're not sure which one you should choose. There are many that can be done, and they all have their pros and cons. It really depends on what you're looking to get out of the contest, and how much effort you want to put into it.

Like to win

A like to win contest asks users to like a photo that you have shared; and liking that photo will enter them into the contest. This type of contest is easy to set up and moderate. You just post a picture and you'll be able to see who liked it and hold a random draw out of those users. As a bonus, if you ask users to 'double tap to like' it may increase your engagement rates. In addition to that, this type of contest can land you on Instagram's Discovery page, which will get you even more exposure.

Comment to win

Like "liking to win", this type of contest runs the same way but users comment on a photo rather than liking it. You can choose winners based on the best comment, or choose one randomly as you do with liking to win. This type of contest can help you gain new followers and increase your engagement.

Repost to win

Repost to win asks users to post a photo you've shared on their own profile. This is great for businesses that want to gain more exposure to other followers but because photos can't be easily shared like they can on Facebook, it can be difficult for users. They'll have to save your photo onto their own phone and then share it. Also, it's important to remember to include a hashtag with these photos, and ask re-posters to do the same, or it will be impossible to track down who shared it.

Tag a photo

Post a photo and ask users to tag someone in it to win. It can get you a lot of exposure because once someone's tagged they may tag someone else so they also have a chance of winning. These contests can also be a great way to identify the users that are really eager to be part of your brand.

Selfie contests

Selfies are great because users think they're really fun and will love posting images of themselves. To increase exposure for your business, ask users to post a selfie while they're using your product. Here it's also important to remember to include a specific hashtag so that it's easy to search for the pictures once the contest is over. It's also important to realize that this type of contest won't be suitable for all businesses.

How long should I run an Instagram contest?

Of course, you want to put a time limit on the contest so that users know when to expect results to be announced and so that you know when you can stop searching through Instagram posts and users. Again, the timeframe you choose will depend on how much effort you want to put into the contest, and what your end goals are.

Daily

Running a contest that lasts for just one day can be fun, and users may be more invested in them because well, they don't have to invest too much in them. However, they can also involve a lot of work for a short timeframe.

One week or less

Running a contest for one week or less increases the urgency factor users will feel when taking part in the contest. It gets people excited for just a few days, and they won't want to be the only one missing out on it. But, that short timeframe will also mean that you don't reach as many people.

Two weeks

Some people consider two weeks to be the perfect timeframe for an Instagram contest. It's long enough that it can get you a lot of exposure, but not so long that people will forget about it and lose interest. But behind the scenes, two weeks may not give you enough time to hit your monthly target so if that's a priority, you need to keep that in mind.

A month or longer

These can generate a lot of interest and get your business maximum exposure. You can also use monthly festivities such as Breast Cancer Awareness Month in October to help promote your contest. But, because it is a longer timeframe, you'll have to put in even more work into it.

What are the best analytical tools for Instagram?

Just like any other type of marketing platform, you want to make sure that you're tracking the results so you can determine whether or not your efforts are paying off or if something needs to be changed. Instagram Insights is a great tool for this that's built right into the app, but there are others that can be used too.

The two main analytic tools are Iconosquare and Totems and both have their pros and cons. Iconosquare is free and provides lots of different features that let you view and browse Instagram right within the tool. It will also provide you with many different tracking measures including growth charts, engagement rates, best times to post, and more.

Totems however, offers just a bit more. It will includes everything Iconosquare does, but also has additional features such as hashtag monitoring and a social CRM. And everything can be viewed within the analytics dashboard. The biggest downside of Totems is that it comes with a high price of $149 a month.

Whether business owners use Instagram Insights, Iconosquare or Totems, the important thing is that they're using something to help track their Instagram marketing campaigns. It's the only way to measure marketing efforts and determine what's working and what's not.

Next Steps

Looking to explode your business? Contact Varinder at:

vinny@socialmediaactive.com